12 AWESOME WOMEN OF SCIENCE YOU'VE NEVER HEARD OF

by Samantha Gouldson

Copyright © 2015 Samantha Gouldson

Cover Illustration by Emily Brady

All rights reserved.

The #12Women Series

**12 Awesome Women Explorers
By Lynn Schreiber**

**12 Awesome Women of Science
By Samantha Gouldson**

To Lex, who showed me that I'm awesome too.

INTRODUCTION

With a contented sigh, Lucy closed the book. She'd learned about so many explorers in the past week, that she was almost looking forward to their next homework assignment. She and her friend Sarah had pored over books from the library, searched YouTube and googled for what seemed like days. Their report had been written, and presented to their school class.

The teacher had frowned when she realised that the girls hadn't chosen one of the suggested explorers, but had come up with their own. Once Lucy had explained that they'd wanted to find out about women explorers, Ms Williams had relented, and soon she was just as engrossed in the story of Gudrid as the rest of the class! Ms Williams had praised them, and even said that she'd be more thoughtful when selecting famous people for future tasks.

As she and Sarah walked out of the history department, then climbed the stairs to the science lab, they talked about the other women they'd discovered while they were researching their project. Some of the explorers they'd found were scientists too, like Louise Boyd, who lead scientific explorations to the North Pole. They decided to ask their science teacher, Miss Duncan if she knew of other women scientists.

"Oh, yes! There were lots of female scientists, but many of them weren't recognised while they were alive', Miss Duncan replied. "One of the women who inspired me to study Chemistry at university was Rosalind Franklin, who really should have received the Nobel Prize for her work! People often think of Marie Curie, when they are asked to name a female scientist, but there were of course many more. Shall I draw up a list?"

"That would be really helpful, Miss Duncan", Lucy smiled in response. "Sarah and I will start searching online, to see if we can find some pictures. Do you think they had to wear those wide, impractical skirts in the lab?"

Miss Duncan frowned, as she searched her bookcase, "I think they'd be quite impractical, particularly when they were doing experiments with combustible materials. And dangerous too. They'd be scolded by the Health and Safety experts, for sure! Ah, here it is. Look, this is Rosalind. No wide skirts in sight, but of course, that wasn't the fashion when she was a young woman".

The girls leaned forward, and gazed at the black and white photograph of a rather earnest looking woman.

EDITH CLARKE

> "There is no demand for women engineers, as such, as there are for women doctors; but there's always a demand for anyone who can do a good piece of work"
>
> Edith Clarke
> Electrical Engineer

Edith Clarke was born in February 1883 in Maryland, USA, one of nine children. Her parents died when she was just 12 years. At school she struggled with reading and spelling, which today would probably be diagnosed as learning difficulties, but she had a great talent for mathematics. When she turned 18 years, she used the inheritance her parents had left her to pay for her studies. In 1908 she graduated from Vassar College with a degree in mathematics and astronomy. At first she taught at a private girls' school, then at Marshall College in West Virginia.

In 1911 she took a summer job as a "computer assistant" at AT&T. In those days "computers" weren't machines but people who could do complex mathematics, in order to *compute* the answer to a problem. Edith found the job so interesting that she stayed on to train more "computers".

In 1918 she left in order to enrol on the electrical engineering course at the renowned Massachusetts Institute of Technology (MIT). She graduated a year later with an MSc in electrical engineering, the first time the department had ever awarded a degree to a woman. Edith was still being held back because she was a woman, and so in 1921 she travelled to Constantinople (now Istanbul), where she taught at the Women's College, and was appointed professor of physics. She returned to America a year later, and was finally given a job as a full engineer.

Edith wrote and published many papers, as well as a textbook for engineering schools and colleges. She invented the Clarke calculator, to improve methods of solving complex power transmission problems, over distances as long as 250 miles. She was particularly skilled at simplifying complicated mathematical problems and translating them into graphs and charts that could be more easily understood. Her skills were vital, as industrial America became increasingly dependent on electricity.

Edith achieved several firsts in her life - she was the first woman to deliver a paper to the American Institute of Electrical Engineers, she was the first woman in the USA to be a professor of electrical engineering, and she was the first woman to be elected as a fellow of the American Institute of Electrical Engineers.

In her early career Edith had been unable to find work as an engineer because she was a woman. By the time she died in 1959 she had proved that women were at least as good at electrical engineering as men, and her example made it easier for more women to qualify and work in that field.

SOPHIE GERMAIN

Born in 1776, Marie Sophie Germain was the daughter of a wealthy merchant. Her mother and sister were both called Marie Madeline, so she may have preferred

Sophie to avoid any more confusion. She grew up during the French Revolution and was just 13 years old when the fall of the Bastille occurred. It was believed to be unsafe for women and girls to venture outside during these revolutionary times, and so the young Sophie was kept indoors. In order to prevent boredom she explored her father's library, becoming fascinated with mathematics, and even teaching herself Latin and Greek so that she could read more about the subject.

Sophie's parents were strongly opposed to her new-found love for mathematics, as it was thought to be an inappropriate subject for a woman. When they discovered that Sophie had been studying in her room at night, they stopped lighting her fire and took away her candles. Not to be deterred, Sophie would wrap herself in quilts and study by the light of candles that she had smuggled into her bedroom. When her parents found her asleep at her desk one bitter morning, her slate covered in mathematical calculations and her ink frozen, they relented and allowed her to study.

When Sophie was 18 years old, a new kind of university, the École Polytechnique, opened in Paris but only men were allowed to study there. The new system meant that lecture notes were available to anyone who asked for them, and so Sophie was able to study at home.

She began to send her work to Joseph Louis Legrange, a famous mathematician and teacher, using the assumed name Monsieur Le Blanc because she feared that she would not be taken seriously, as a woman mathematician. Legrange was so impressed that he requested a meeting with the young "man", so Sophie had to reveal her true identity. Althought very surprised, Legrange, didn't mind that she was a woman, and indeed became her mentor.

Sophie continued to study mathematics, and in 1816 she was awarded a prize for her work on elasticity by the Académie des Sciences. She was the first woman to attend its sessions without being married to a member of the Académie.

She is best known for her work on number theory, particularly that related to Fermat's Last Theorem, which is a really difficult maths problem that wasn't solved for 357 years. Her work laid the foundations for applied mathematics as it is used today, including in calculations when constructing tall buildings, as well as contributing significantly to mathematical physics, which was a new field of study at the time.

Sophie died in 1831 and was buried in Père Lachaise cemetery in Paris, where her grave is often still visited by students of mathematics.

ALICE C EVANS

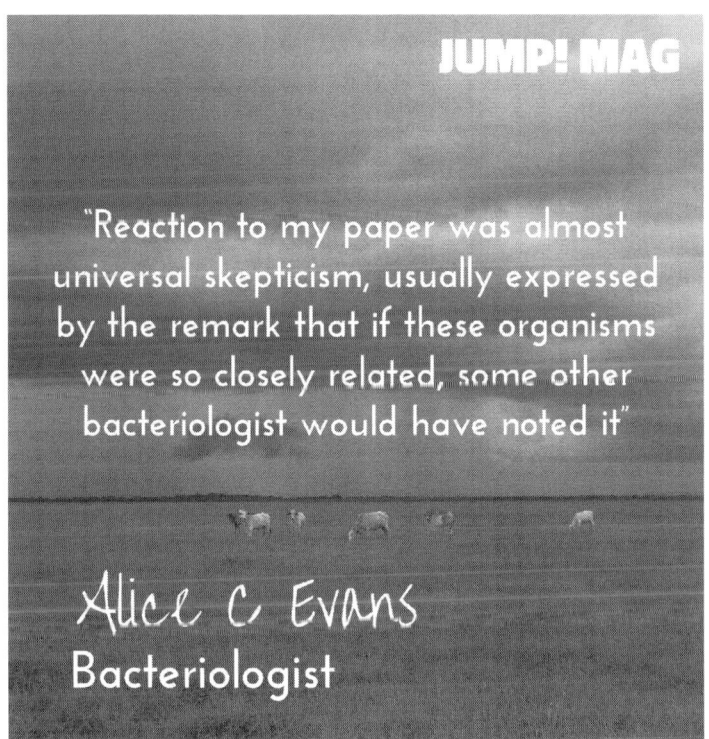

You probably haven't heard of Alice Catherine Evans but if you like drinking milk, then she's had a big impact on your life. She was born on a farm in 1881 in

Pennsylvania, USA, and in 1901 she started working as an elementary school teacher because she couldn't afford to go to college.

When Cornell University offered rural teachers the chance to take a course on nature she immediately signed up. At the same time she took an introductory course at the Agricultural College. This led to her winning a scholarship to Cornell University, and she graduated from there in 1909 with a bachelors degree in bacteriology (the study of bacteria).

She then became the first woman to be offered a scholarship by the University of Wisconsin, where in 1910 she graduated with a masters degree in bacteriology.

Alice became one of the first women to hold a permanent position at the US Department of Agriculture, in the Bureau of Animal Husbandry. She worked in the dairy division, studying bacteria in milk and cheese.

In 1918 she published a paper showing that drinking milk which hadn't been pasteurised (heated to kill the bacteria) could lead to a disease called *brucellosis* being passed from cows to humans. Brucellosis was also known as undulent fever, and was an unpleasant illness, causing fevers, weight loss, headaches, extreme tiredness and joint pain.

Unfortunately Alice's paper wasn't taken seriously by the scientific community. Not only did she not have a PhD, she was also a woman and these two things meant that her research was dismissed.

By the late 1920s other scientists around the world had come to the same conclusions as Alice, and the pasteurisation of milk became a requirement in many countries. Alice's research meant that countless people were prevented from contracting this painful illness. Sadly Alice wasn't one of them, as she contracted chronic brucellosis in 1922 while carrying out her studies. The disease never left her system and she suffered from recurring bouts for the rest of her life.

After leaving the Department of Agriculture, Alice worked for the US Hygienic Laboratory, researching infectious diseases such as meningitis. She became the first woman president of the American Society of

Bacteriologists and after her retirement in 1945, she lectured to women about career development, and encouraged them to pursue a career in science. Alice died in 1975 aged 94 years

WANG ZHENYI

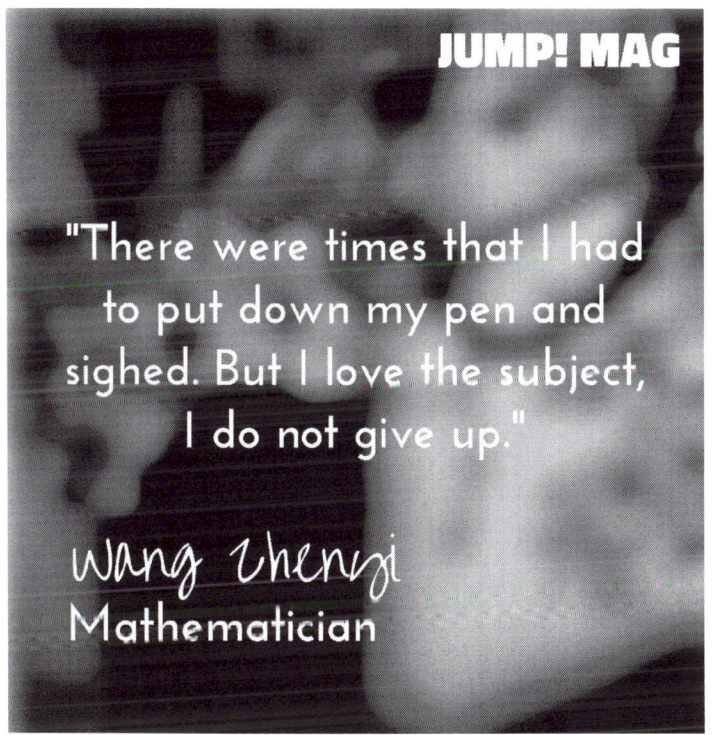

Wang Zhenyi was born in 1768, and was an accomplished scholar, specialising in astronomy and mathematics. Unusually for the time she learned to read at an early age. Her grandfather had a library containing over 70 books. At that time books were expensive and rare, so this collection was very impressive. From her father and grandfather she learned astronomy, geography, medicine and mathematics, and from her grandmother she learned poetry. She travelled extensively with her father, and on one of these trips, she learned martial arts, archery and how to ride a horse from the wife of a Mongolian general.

Zhenyi strongly believed that mathematics and science should be accessible to all people, whatever their background or gender. At the time most mathematical texts were written in the aristocratic language of the Qing dynasty, so Zhenyi translated and simplified them so that more people could learn.

In doing this she also simplified many important mathematical equations and proofs. She wrote a short paper explaining gravity in simple terms, and why no-one falls off the Earth even though it's a sphere.

Zhenyi's greatest contribution to science was her explanation of eclipses. In 18th century China many people still believed that an eclipse was a sign that the gods were angry, but Zhenyi proved that it was due to the Moon coming between the Earth and the Sun.

She did this by arranging objects to mimic the behaviour of these planetary bodies. A round table represented the Earth, a lamp was the Sun and a round mirror was the moon. By moving these objects in the same way as their counterparts move through the sky, she was able to prove that a solar eclipse occurs because the Moon moves between the Earth and the Sun. In the same way she showed that a lunar eclipse occurs when the Earth is between the Sun and Moon.

Beside her scientific work, Zhenyi was an accomplished poet, and believed in the equality of men and women, writing

It's made to believe,

Women are the same as Men;

Are you not convinced,

Daughters can also be heroic?

Sadly Zhenyi died at just 29 years of age, but when she knew she was dying, she passed her work on to her best friend Madam Kuai, who left them to her nephew, renowned scholar Qian Yiji. He compiled Wang Zhenyi's works into *Shusuan jiancun* or Simple Principles of Calculation.

Her contribution to science and mathematics is still remembered today; in 1994 the International Astronomical Union named a crater on Venus after her.

DOROTHY HODGKIN

Dorothy Crowfoot Hodgkin was born in Cairo, Egypt in 1910. Her parents were both British archaeologists and Dorothy spent the first few years of her life living in

Cairo. When World War I began, Dorothy and her sisters were left in the care of relatives in England while her parents returned to Egypt. She never lived with her parents in Egypt again, although they visited her each summer and her mother returned to Britain for a year when Dorothy was eight years old.

When Dorothy was ten, she visited a family friend in Sudan who allowed her to study and analyse chemicals. This sparked her interest and she became one of only two girls permitted to study chemistry with the boys at her school.

At the age of 13, she visited her parents and helped with an archaeological excavation. She and her sister used a portable mineral analysis kit to study the pebbles and stones they found, which Dorothy found fascinating.

She was tempted to pursue a career in archaeology until she was given a copy of a book called "Concerning The Nature Of Things" when she was 15. This explained how it was possible to examine the structure of chemicals using x-rays and she was intrigued.

At Oxford University, Dorothy combined her love of

archaeology and chemistry, analysing glass tesserae from Jerash, an ancient city in Jordan, in her first year, but she soon became focused solely on chemistry and obtained her first degree. She gained her doctorate degree at Cambridge University.

In 1934 she moved back to Oxford, where she became a lecturer in chemistry. Not only was she one of the first female lecturers at Oxford University to marry and have children, she was the first woman to ever receive maternity pay from the university. During the 1940s one of her students was Margaret Roberts, later the first female British prime minister Margaret Thatcher.

During her career Dorothy worked on x-ray crystallography, a technique that allowed scientists to work out how proteins were structured. First the chemicals had to be crystallised, then frozen to prevent them cracking. Then they were x-rayed, and the pattern that they gave off helped scientists figure out the shape and structure of the protein. This is important to know because then scientists can examine how the protein interacts with drugs and other biological molecules.

As Dorothy herself once remarked

"A great advantage of x-ray analysis as a method of chemical structure analysis is its power to show some totally unexpected and surprising structure with, at the same time, complete certainty".

After being diagnosed with rheumatoid arthritis at just 24 years, Dorothy had to spend increasing amounts of time in a wheelchair. She didn't allow this to interfere with her research, and continued to improve and refine x-ray crystallography. This enabled her to discover the structure of proteins including penicillin and insulin as well as vitamin B12.

It was this third discovery that won her the Nobel Prize for Chemistry in 1964, and she remains the only British woman to have ever won this award.

TESSY THOMAS

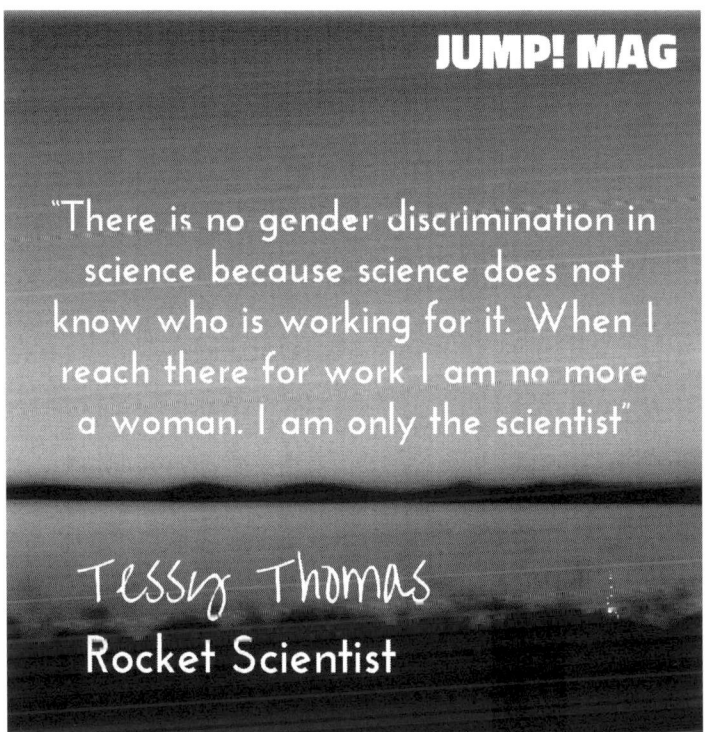

Tessy Thomas is frequently called The Missile Woman or Agni Putri (meaning "one born of fire"). She was born in the Indian municipality of Alappuzha in 1963

and grew up near a rocket-launching station, and says that this sparked her fascination with rockets and missiles.

After Tessy finished school she studied for her Bachelor degree at Thissur Engineering College in Calicut, before moving to the western Indian city of Pune to obtain her Masters degree in guided missiles.

In 1988, at the age of 25, Tessy began working for India's Defence Research and Development Organisation (DRDO). She had also applied for a job with the Indian Administrative Service but the DRDO offered her a job first. Her focus was the Agni nuclear missile programme, named after the Hindu god of fire. The Agni series are long-range ballistic missiles, which means that although they are initially guided after firing they then rely on gravity to bring them down onto the target.

Tessy was the associate project director of the AgniIII missile project, and project director for both the AgniIV and AgniV missiles. She's currently based at the Advanced Systems Laboratory in Hyderabad. As head of the team she works 12 hours a day, 7 days a week.

The missiles not only have to be designed, developed and built but also tested in simulators thousands of times. Only then can they be test-fired.

In 2012 Tessy was given the Lal Bahadur Shastri National Award for her outstanding contribution to India's missile technology. Although her parents named her after Mother Teresa, the Roman Catholic nun and Nobel Peace Prize winner who worked with the poor in Calcutta, Tessy has no qualms about creating nuclear missiles.

"I have built a vehicle that can also carry flowers. I am building it for a country that only wants it as a deterrent. So I am building it to actually ensure peace in this region."

SHIRLEY ANN JACKSON

> "Treasure your curiosity and nurture your imagination. Have confidence in yourself. Do not let others put limits on you. Dare to imagine the unimaginable."
>
> *Shirley Ann Jackson*
> Physicist
>
> — JUMP! MAG

Shirley was born in Washington DC, in 1946. Her parents supported her studies and encouraged her interest in science projects, even the one where she collected bees in 30 jars and kept them alive by feeding them sugar! She also built go-karts with her sister Gloria, which led to a lifelong interest in how things work.

In 1964 Shirley left high school and began her studies at the Massachusetts Institute of Technology (MIT). After gaining her bachelor's degree in 1968 she stayed on to study for her doctorate, which she gained in 1973. She was the first woman of colour to be awarded a doctorate by MIT, and only the second woman of colour to be awarded a doctorate in physics in the whole of the USA. The first was Willie Hobbs Moore, in 1972.

During the first half of the 1970s Shirley's research focused on subatomic particles, which are tiny pieces of matter smaller than atoms. She worked at a number of prestigious laboratories across the USA and in Europe, and was one of few women in her field, and of even fewer women of colour. As she later told *Science* Magazine,

"If you give a physics paper, it had better be good, because people will remember."

In 1976 she began working for Bell Telephone laboratories, and the research she conducted enabled other scientists to later invent the touchtone telephone, solar cells, fibre optic cables and more.

Shirley has taught many students, and has written or collaborated on over 100 scientific papers. She has also held many positions of authority, including the presidency of several scientific associations, and Chair of the Nuclear Regulatory Committee in the 1990s. Today Shirley is the president of the Rensselaer Polytechnic Institute, the oldest technological research university in the USA, and in addition to her doctorate from MIT she has been awarded 52 honorary degrees!

WU CHIENSHIUNG

> 'I sincerely doubt, that any open-minded person really believes in the notion that women have no intellectual capacity for science and technology.'
>
> *Wu ChienShiung*
> Physicist

ChienShiung was born in Liuhe, Jiangsu province in China in 1912. Her father was a former engineer who ran a girls' school and her mother was a teacher. Both her parents encouraged her interests in mathematics and science, which she studied herself as they weren't part of the curriculum at the school she was attending. In 1934 she graduated from the National Central University of Nanking (now Nanjing) with a bachelors degree in physics.

For the next couple of years ChienShiung taught and researched at the National Central University, but there were no senior positions in physics in China at that time.

In 1936, with money from her uncle, and the support of her parents she moved to the USA. She enrolled at the University of California, Berkeley and in 1940 received her doctorate degree.

During this time, there was a civil war in China. After the Communist Party came to power, Chien-Shiung's father wrote to warn her that it was too dangerous for her to return. In 1954 she became a US citizen, which meant she was banned from entering China. Wu Chien-Shiung didn't see her family again, although was eventually able to visit to her home country and meet some of her relatives.

Between 1942 and 1944 ChienShiung taught physics to naval officers at Princeton University, the first woman to teach male students there. In 1944 she was invited to work on the top-secret Manhattan Project, where she developed a way of enriching uranium ore that produced large amounts of fuel for the atomic bomb.

After World War II was over ChienShiung worked as a research assistant at Columbia University and was appointed an associate professor in 1952.

In 1957 ChienShiung and two colleagues proved that a widely accepted "law" of physics was wrong. For this work her male colleagues were awarded the Nobel Prize for Physics, but ChienShiung was not.

She continued her research at Columbia and worked to improve Geiger counters, a way of detecting nuclear radiation. ChienShiung became a full professor in 1958, and she remained at Columbia until her retirement in 1981.

She was the first woman to receive an honorary doctorate from Princeton University and the first woman to be president of the American Physical Society. She was also the first living scientist to have an asteroid named after her; 2752 Wu ChienShiung.

After her retirement ChienShiung lectured widely, encouraging young women with an interest in science. She died in 1997.

NETTIE STEVENS

> "How could you think your questions would bother me? They never will, so long as I keep my enthusiasm for biology; and that, I hope, will be as long as I live."
>
> *Nettie Stevens*
> Geneticist
>
> — JUMP! MAG

Nettie was born in 1861 in Vermont, USA. Although it was then quite unusual for women to be educated, she attended the Westford Academy, where she was one of the most talented students. When she left at age 19 she became a teacher, one of the few professions open to women at that time. She taught for years, saving her money so that she could eventually go to university. She graduated from Leland Stanford University with a bachelors degree in 1899 and her masters degree in 1900. In 1903, she received her doctorate from Bryn Mawr College.

Nettie's determination paid off, and she became an extremely busy research scientist. She was particularly interested in chromosomes, the tiny structures within our cells that were known to determine things about us like our eye colour, skin colour and height. At that time, it was not known that chromosomes are also responsible for determining the sex of a person, i.e. if a baby is born a boy or a girl.

She was studying mealworms when she noticed that the males made reproductive cells (sperm) with both X and Y chromosomes, whereas female reproductive cells (eggs) only had X chromosomes. She concluded, correctly, that it is the male who determines the sex of the offspring and that it is the chromosomes that carry this information.

This was a truly groundbreaking discovery. Until then, it was widely accepted in the scientific community that the sex of an infant was determined by the mother, possibly with the influence of environmental factors.

Nettie's work was largely ignored, despite another scientist called Edmund Beecher Wilson coming to similar conclusions. Nettie's work was more advanced, and Wilson later reissued his paper thanking Nettie for her discoveries and influence. Despite Wilson's acknowledgement, it is he who is best known for the discovery of sex determination in cells, not Nettie. Nettie died in 1912, when she was 50 years old. .

LISE MEITNER

> "Life need not be easy, if it is meaningful
>
> Lise Meitner
> Physicist
>
> — JUMP! MAG

Lise was born in the Austrian capital, Vienna in 1878, and was interested in science from a young age. Her sister Frida was later interviewed on the radio, and said that when Lise was eight years old, she slept with her maths book under her pillow. Lise wasn't one for doing the housework, Frida explained, "Lise can't do that. It isn't in the physics books!"

Their parents supported Lise's interest in physics, but because of restrictions on female education she wasn't able to begin university until she was 23 years old. She received her doctorate in physics in 1905, only the second woman to do so at the University of Vienna. The only offer of work she received was from a gas lamp factory, so with her parents' support and money, she travelled to Berlin. There she studied with the eminent physicist Max Planck, and began working with chemist Otto Hahn.

Lise and Hahn continued their work at the newly established Kaiser Wilhelm Institut in Berlin, but Lise wasn't paid for her work until 1913, when she was offered a job by the University of Prague. She turned them down but the offer prompted a counteroffer of a permanent position by the Kaiser Wilhelm Institut. At the age of 35 years, Lise was finally receiving a salary for her work!

In 1922 Lise discovered something called the Auger effect, a particular type of electron emission. However it was named after a French scientist, Pierre Victor Auger, who "discovered" it a year later. In 1926 Lise became the first woman in Germany to become a professor of physics.

Although Lise was born into a Jewish family she had converted to Christianity when she was in her thirties. In 1930s Germany, with the rise of Hitler and the Nazi Party, her Jewish ancestry meant she was in danger, and in 1938 she fled the country, travelling first to the Netherlands and then on to Sweden. With barely any resources or equipment she continued her research, corresponding with Hahn and other German colleagues, as well as working with the famous physicist Niels Bohr. In late 1938, Lise met Otto Hahn in Copenhagen to conduct secret experiments.

In January 1939 Otto Hahn, together with a chemist called Strassmann, published the evidence for nuclear fission. This is the process of splitting an atom into two or more parts, which until then was believed to be impossible. They didn't understand why it happened until February 1939, when Lise and her nephew, physicist Otto Frisch, published their paper explaining the process, and giving it the name 'nuclear fission'.

Albert Einstein had been following Lise's work with interest, and even called her "the German Marie Curie", but now he wrote to the American president, Franklin Roosevelt, warning that it was now possible for the Germans to develop an atomic bomb. This led to the Manhattan Project, and the creation of the atomic bomb by the USA, Canada and the UK. Lise refused to work on the project, and was devastated when she heard of the bombing of Hiroshima.

In 1944 Hahn was awarded the Nobel Prize for Chemistry for his work on nuclear fission, but Lise was never mentioned. Lise continued working, and was involved in the creation of one of the first peacetime nuclear reactors.

After her retirement in 1960, she moved to UK, where many of her relatives lived. She died in 1968, with her work still largely unrecognised.

In 1997 element 109 in the periodic table was officially named Meitnerium, after Lise. It remains the only element to be named after a woman who existed instead of being mythological.

ROSALIND FRANKLIN

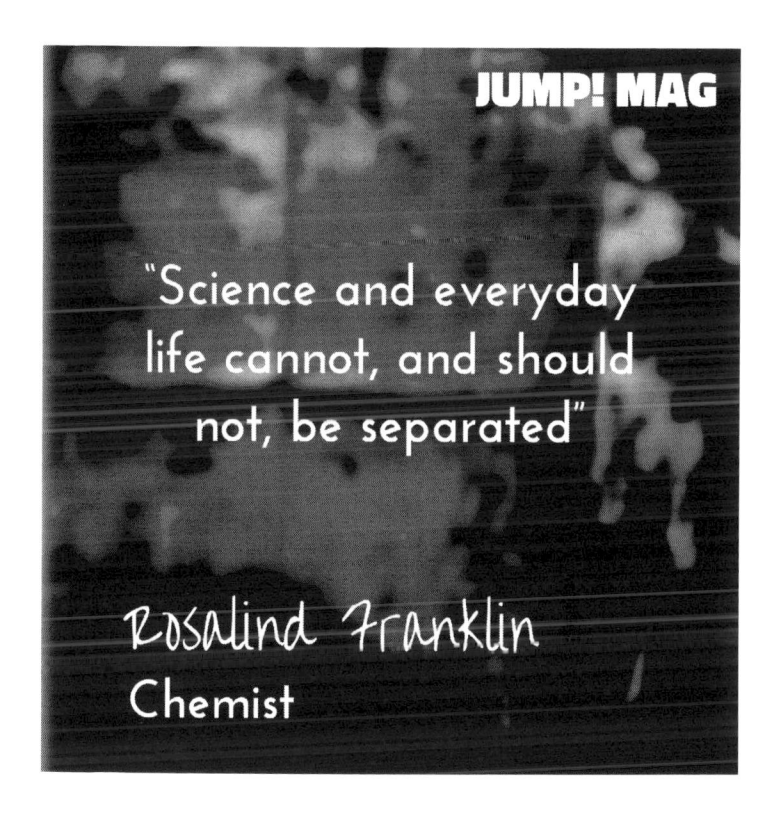

> "Science and everyday life cannot, and should not, be separated"
>
> *Rosalind Franklin*
> Chemist

Rosalind Elsie Franklin was born in London in 1920. Her family was wealthy and very active in public life. Her father was a banker, a great uncle was in government, and one of her aunts was involved in the women's suffrage movement, and campaigned for women to be given the right to vote. Rosalind first became interested in science while at school, and by the age of 15 had decided to become a chemist.

Rosalind began her studies at Newham College, Cambridge in 1938, graduating in 1941. In 1942 she began working at the British Coal Utilisation Research Association, studying carbon and graphite microstructures, which means how the substances looked when examined through a powerful microscope. In 1945 she received a doctorate in physical chemistry from Cambridge University.

For three years Rosalind worked in France, learning and developing X-ray crystallography, which is a way of studying the structure of proteins, but in 1951 she returned to UK and took up a job at King's College London. Her new area of interest was DNA, a long thin molecule that contains the instructions telling our bodies how to develop and function.

At the time no one knew what this mysterious molecule looked like, and different methods of examining it had produced different theories. Other scientists, including Maurice Wilkins, Francis Crick and James Watson, were also working on the problem and there was quite a lot of competition to be the first with a breakthrough.

Rosalind worked hard and was very close to solving the problem of how DNA was structured, but Wilkins showed Crick and Watson some of Rosalind's photographs of DNA without her permission, and this led to them publishing their conclusions just before her. Their work was widely celebrated while Rosalind's work was only seen as supporting theirs, not as the groundbreaking work that had led to the discovery.

In 1953 Rosalind moved to Birkbeck College, London and began studying viruses. She died in 1958, aged only 37. In 1962 Watson, Crick and Wilkins were awarded the Nobel Prize for Physiology and Medicine for their work on DNA.

James Watson later suggested that because only three people can receive the same Nobel Prize, Rosalind and Wilkins should have received the prize for Chemistry; he and Crick could have been awarded the Nobel Prize for Physiology or Medicine.

Rosalind's exclusion is due in part to the fact that Nobel Prizes cannot be awarded posthumously, but the fact remains that not only was she never nominated, none of her colleagues even mentioned her significance.

MARIA GOEPPERTMAYER

> "Winning the Nobel Prize wasn't half as exciting as doing the work itself"
>
> Maria Goeppert Mayer
> Physicist
>
> JUMP! MAG

Maria was born in 1906 in Kattowitz, Germany, which is now in Poland, and called Katowice. Her father was a professor at the University of Göttingen and with the support of her parents she studied mathematics and science. In 1924 she began her studies at the University of Göttingen, initially in mathematics but switching to physics as she became interested in the ideas of renowned physicists Niels Bohr and Max Born. She received her doctorate in 1930. In the same year she married Joseph Mayer and moved to the USA.

Maria continued to work as a physicist, although it was difficult for her to find a paid job because female scientists weren't taken seriously. For years she held unofficial and unpaid positions at a number of universities, as well as teaching science at colleges.

In 1941 she joined the Manhattan Project, the research project that led to the creation of the first atomic bombs during World War II. Finally, in 1946, she was offered a part-time job as Senior Physicist in the Theoretical Physics Division of the Argonne National Laboratory. This was the first time that she had a job where the salary was what you would expect for someone of her training and experience.

During her time at Argonne, Maria studied the structure of elements. The model of the atom already suggested that the electrons moved in "shells" as they orbited the nucleus, but Maria was one of the first to realise that inside the nucleus, the centre of an atom, the particles tended to be arranged in pairs, and rotated in closed layers.

She explained the idea like this:

"Think of a room full of waltzers. Suppose they go round the room in circles, each circle enclosed within another. Then imagine that in each circle, you can fit twice as many dancers by having one pair go clockwise and another pair go counterclockwise. Then add one more variation; all the dancers are spinning twirling round and round like tops as they circle the room, each pair both twirling and circling".

Several other researchers reached the same conclusions independently of Maria and in 1963, alongside J Hans Jensen and Eugene Wigner, Maria was awarded the Nobel Prize for Physics for her work on atomic shell structure.

JUMP! BOOKS

The InstaExplorer Series - by Millie Slavidou

The Olympias Clue

The first book in a series of adventure stories for kids, featuring intrepid explorer Lucy Evans. Armed with her trusty smartphone, her wits and an adventurous spirit, Lucy sets out to solve mysteries, explore foreign countries and cultures, and meet interesting people around the world. Her journey begins in a small town in Greece, where between sending messages to her friends back home, and exploring her new home, Lucy makes an intriguing discovery in an overgrown park.

Dragon's Rock

Fresh from her incredible first adventure, Lucy heads to Wales and falls feet first into another mystery. A missing businesswoman, a lost handbag, a tumbledown castle ... Lucy will have to work fast to save the day!

Christmas in Greece

British teen Lucy is settling into her new life abroad, learning the language and making new friends in school. During the festive season, Lucy discovers the very different Christmas traditions, and joins in with the local celebrations. The author Millie Slavidou draws on her personal experience, as a British woman in Greece, to explore the traditions and heritage of the country.

Carnival in Germany

In the fourth book of the InstaExplorer series, we continue the theme of experiencing local culture and take a trip with Lucy Evans to the German city of Würzburg, to attend the yearly carnival. Lucy and her friend visit tourist attractions and take part in the celebrations, sharing updates with their friends via social media. Readers can enjoy the Instagram-style illustrations while learning about about the history and traditions of the Franconian city.

12 Awesome Women Explorers You've Never Heard Of - by Lynn Schreiber

The first in a series of non-fiction books for kids, highlighting the achievements and legacies of women you've never heard of! Follow in the footsteps of twelve awesome women, as they walk, run, ski and sail around the earth, fly into the sky, and rocket into outer space. From modern and ancient times, these women from different walks of life share a thirst for knowledge, a brave heart, and a yearning to explore.

12 Science Words That Don't Mean What You Think They Do - by Samantha Gouldson

"He has a theory, but he has no proof, that his solution is the right one".

We use lots of scientific words and phrases in everyday language. Often their usage changes, until their everyday meanings have become completely muddled, and are very different to their scientific definition. Why is a "theory" not just a good idea, and when we ask a scientist for "proof", why can it never be incontestable? This book is aimed at tweens and teens, and explains the difference between the scientific and the everyday meanings of various words.

Printed in Great Britain
by Amazon.co.uk, Ltd.,
Marston Gate.